The Best 20 Ideas for Making Money Online

Arthur Anderson

Published by Arthur Anderson, 2023.

While every precaution has been taken in the preparation of this book, the publisher assumes no responsibility for errors or omissions, or for damages resulting from the use of the information contained herein.

THE BEST 20 IDEAS FOR MAKING MONEY ONLINE

First edition. July 29, 2023.

ISBN: 979-8223807490

Written by Arthur Anderson.

The Best 20 Ideas for Making Money Online

Arthur Anderson

Affiliate Marketing

Promoting products or services from other companies and earning commissions for each sale or action made through your affiliate link.

Affiliate marketing is an online marketing strategy in which an affiliate promotes products or services from another company and receives a commission for each sale or action generated through their affiliate link. Here are 30 detailed ways to do affiliate marketing:

Review content: Write detailed reviews of relevant products or services in your niche, highlighting their features, benefits, and potential uses.

Thematic blogs: Create a blog specialized in a specific topic and share useful and valuable content, linking related products with your recommendations.

Influencer marketing: If you have a follower base on social media, promote products through your profiles and use affiliate links.

YouTube videos: Create tutorials, unboxing videos, comparisons, or product reviews and add affiliate links in the description.

Email marketing: Build a list of subscribers interested in your niche and send them emails with recommendations and affiliate links.

Lead magnets: Offer free high-quality content (eBooks, guides, courses) and promote related products within the material.

Coupons and discounts: Provide exclusive discount codes to your followers and earn commissions on sales.

Webinars and online events: Organize webinars on relevant topics and recommend useful products during the presentation.

Informative infographics: Create attractive infographics on niche topics and link related products in them.

Comparisons and product tables: Compare different products or services and help your audience make informed decisions.

Paid advertising: Use paid ads on social media and search engines to promote affiliate products.

Contests and giveaways: Organize giveaways where the prize includes products you are promoting through your affiliate links.

Guest posting: Write guest posts on other blogs and strategically place affiliate links within the content.

Evergreen content marketing: Create evergreen (always relevant) content that will continue to generate income over time.

Podcasts: If you have a podcast, mention and promote related products in your episodes.

Testimonials and personal experiences: Share your personal experiences with products or services you have used and link through your testimonials.

Recommended resources and tools: Create a page with your favorite tools and resources and link them with your affiliate links.

Recommendations in forums and groups: Participate in online communities related to your niche and offer helpful recommendations with affiliate links when appropriate.

Retargeting: Use retargeting campaigns to show product ads to people who have already visited your website.

SEO: Optimize your content for search engines, which can generate organic traffic to your affiliate links.

eBooks and digital books: Create and sell your own eBooks related to the niche, including relevant affiliate links.

Product compilations: Create lists of the best products in a specific category and link to each of them.

Sponsored posts: Collaborate with other companies and brands to promote their products in exchange for an affiliate commission.

Social media posts: Share relevant content on your social media and link affiliate products in your posts.

Resource pages: Create pages on your website with links to resources and products you recommend.

Thank-you pages: After someone subscribes or makes a purchase through your affiliate link, redirect them to a thank-you page with more recommendations.

Newsletter: Create a newsletter where you share the latest updates and promotions of affiliate products.

In-person retreats and events: If you organize in-person events, take the opportunity to promote relevant affiliate products.

Integration of links in educational content: Utilize educational content to link to useful affiliate products.

Podcast mentions: If you have a podcast, mention and promote products related to your audience.

Online courses

Create and sell courses on topics you have experience and expertise in.

Creation of tutorial videos: Record presentations or demonstrations in video to visually and clearly explain course content.

Downloadable materials: Provide guides, eBooks, or useful files that students can download to complement their studies.

Live interaction: Conduct live Q&A sessions via streaming platforms to encourage participation and clarify doubts.

Discussion forums: Create a space where students can interact, ask questions, and share ideas.

Exercises and assignments: Assign practical activities for students to apply what they have learned and reinforce their knowledge.

Quizzes and exams: Administer tests to assess students' progress and ensure they have understood the course material.

Gamification: Add gamification elements like points, badges, or levels to increase motivation and student engagement.

Case studies: Use real examples and practical situations to illustrate concepts and applications of the course content.

Webinars and online conferences: Invite experts or professionals in the field to offer talks and share additional knowledge.

Self-assessment: Allow students to evaluate their own progress and understanding of the course content.

Personalized feedback: Provide individualized feedback to students on their performance and areas for improvement.

Student surveys and feedback: Ask for student opinions to improve the course and tailor it to their needs.

Integration of multimedia: Incorporate images, infographics, audios, and other media to enrich the course content.

Personalized coaching and tutoring: Offer one-on-one sessions to address questions and provide additional support.

Escalated content: Divide the course into modules or sections so that students can progress step by step.

Lifetime access to materials: Allow students to access the course content even after completion.

Translations and subtitles: Offer options for students to follow the course in different languages or with subtitles.

Student collaboration: Encourage teamwork and collaboration among students through joint projects.

Certificates and recognition: Award completion certificates or special recognition to students who successfully complete the course.

Updated content: Keep the course up to date with the latest trends and developments in the field.

Mobile access: Ensure the course is accessible from mobile devices for students' convenience.

Audience segmentation: Adapt the course content to different levels of skill or experience.

Affiliate program: Implement a program that allows others to promote your course in exchange for a commission.

Discounts and special offers: Offer temporary promotions to incentivize new student enrollment.

Free sample content: Provide a free introduction to the course so that students can preview the content before enrolling.

Constant course performance evaluation: Analyze metrics and student feedback to make continuous improvements.

Promotion on social media and blogs: Use social media platforms and collaborate with bloggers to promote your course.

Integration with other platforms: Offer the ability to integrate the course with popular learning management tools and platforms.

Online events: Organize special events, such as webinars or live streams, to increase visibility and interest in the course.

Updates and course expansions: Consider adding additional modules or updating content to attract returning students.

Sale of Digital Products:

Offer e-books, music, templates, or downloadable digital resources.

Native iOS Development (Swift):

Use the Swift programming language and Xcode development environment to create applications for Apple devices.

Native Android Development (Java/Kotlin):

Use Java or Kotlin with Android Studio to create applications for Android devices.

Hybrid Development (Flutter):

Use Flutter, a Google framework, to develop applications that run on both iOS and Android with a shared codebase.

Web Development (HTML, CSS, JavaScript):

Create web applications using standard technologies like HTML, CSS, and JavaScript to be accessible through browsers.

Desktop Applications (C#/Java):

Develop desktop software using C# and .NET or Java for cross-platform applications.

macOS App Development (Swift/Objective-C):

Use Swift or Objective-C with Xcode to develop native macOS applications.

Windows App Development (C#):

Use C# and .NET with Visual Studio to create applications for the Windows operating system.

Linux App Development (Python):

Use Python and libraries like GTK or Qt to develop applications for the Linux operating system.

Cloud Applications (AWS, Azure):

Create cloud applications using service providers like Amazon Web Services (AWS) or Microsoft Azure.

Game Development (Unity, Unreal Engine):

Use game engines like Unity or Unreal Engine to develop video games for multiple platforms.

IoT Applications (Internet of Things):

Develop applications that interact with internet-connected devices, such as sensors or actuators.

Augmented Reality (AR) Applications:

Create applications that combine the real world with digital elements using AR technologies like ARKit or ARCore.

Virtual Reality (VR) Applications:

Develop immersive experiences using virtual reality technology like Oculus SDK or SteamVR.

Chatbot Development (Python, Node.js):

Create chatbots that use programming languages like Python or Node.js to interact with users.

Image Processing Applications (OpenCV):

Use the OpenCV library to develop applications that process images and videos.

Machine Learning Applications (TensorFlow, scikit-learn):

Develop applications that utilize machine learning algorithms like TensorFlow or scikit-learn.

Natural Language Processing (NLTK, spaCy) Applications:

Create applications that work with natural language processing using libraries like NLTK or spaCy.

Database Management Systems (MySQL, PostgreSQL):

Develop database management systems using technologies like MySQL or PostgreSQL.

Version Control Systems (Git):

Use Git to manage version control of your code and collaborate with other developers.

E-commerce Applications (WooCommerce, Shopify):

Create online stores using platforms like WooCommerce for WordPress or Shopify.

Social Media Applications (React Native, Firebase):

Develop social media applications using React Native as the frontend and Firebase for database management and authentication.

Data Tracking and Analysis Applications (Google Analytics):

Create applications that collect and analyze user data using tools like Google Analytics.

Security and Encryption Applications (OpenSSL):

Develop applications that ensure data security and encryption using libraries like OpenSSL.

Browser Extensions (JavaScript):

Create web browser extensions using JavaScript to add additional functionalities.

Speech-to-Text Applications:

Develop applications that convert speech into text using speech recognition services.

Remote Control Applications (Bluetooth, Wi-Fi):

Create applications that allow controlling devices or systems through Bluetooth or Wi-Fi.

Geolocation Applications (Google Maps API):

Develop applications that use the Google Maps API to display and work with geographical information.

Data Analysis Applications (Pandas, D3.js):

Create applications that analyze and visualize data using libraries like Pandas and D3.js.

Automation Applications (Python, Selenium):

Develop applications that automate repetitive tasks using Python and the Selenium library.

Mixed Reality Applications (Microsoft HoloLens):

Create applications that combine elements of virtual reality and augmented reality using technology like Microsoft HoloLens.

Blogging

Start a blog about a topic of your interest and monetize it through advertising, sponsorships, and affiliate marketing.

Identify your audience: Before you begin, clearly define who you will be targeting with your blog. Identifying your audience will help you create relevant and engaging content.

Choose a platform: There are several options for creating a blog, such as WordPress, Blogger, or Tumblr. Choose the one that best suits your needs and technical abilities.

Attractive and user-friendly design: Create a clean, appealing, and easy-to-navigate design. Use colors and fonts consistent with the theme of your blog.

Research and plan your content: Conduct thorough research on the topics you want to address on your blog. Plan an editorial calendar to maintain a steady flow of content.

Write original and quality content: Aim to provide unique and valuable content for your readers. Avoid copying and pasting information from other sites.

Optimize for SEO: Learn basic SEO techniques (Search Engine Optimization) to improve the visibility of your blog in search engines.

Use high-quality images: Accompany your posts with attractive and relevant images. You can use free image banks or take your own photographs.

Interact with your readers: Respond to your readers' comments and encourage engagement. This will create a community around your blog.

Promote on social media: Share your posts on social media to expand your reach and attract more traffic to your blog.

Include internal and external links: Link your own related posts and also credible external sources to support your claims.

Use compelling headlines: Headlines are essential for capturing readers' attention. Create interesting and clear titles that reflect the content of your posts.

Mind spelling and grammar: A blog with grammatical and spelling errors can be unappealing to readers. Always review your texts before publishing them.

Offer multimedia content: In addition to images, consider adding videos, infographics, or podcasts to enrich your content.

Participate in blogging communities: Join groups and forums related to your blog's theme to connect with other bloggers and share your posts.

Update regularly: Keep your blog updated with new content. Readers come back if they know they will find fresh information.

Create a newsletter: Offer your readers the option to subscribe to a newsletter to receive the latest updates and news.

Monetize your blog: If you want to generate income with your blog, research affiliate programs, advertising, or selling your own products.

Track your traffic: Use tools like Google Analytics to understand how readers interact with your blog and which content is more popular.

Invite collaborators: Consider inviting experts in the field to write as guest authors on your blog. This will bring diversity and different perspectives.

Create tutorials and guides: People search for solutions and answers online. Provide step-by-step tutorials and guides to help your readers.

Organize contests and giveaways: These activities can generate excitement and increase reader participation on your blog.

Publish interviews: Conduct interviews with relevant people in your industry or niche. This can add value to your content.

Compilations and lists: List-format posts or compilations are very popular. For example, "The Top 10 Tips for..."

Do guest posting: Write guest posts on other relevant blogs to increase your visibility and attract new readers.

Create a series of posts: Organize a series of articles on a specific topic to keep readers interested and looking forward to the next installment.

Conduct surveys and quizzes: Ask your readers for their opinions on important topics or future posts.

Collect testimonials: Ask your readers to share their experiences or testimonials related to your blog. This can increase trust in your content.

Share your experiences: Readers like to feel connected to you. Share your experiences, successes, and challenges in your blogging journey.

Be consistent: Maintain a consistent posting frequency so that readers know when to expect new content.

Analyze and improve: Regularly review your blog's performance and reader feedback. Learn from the data and adjust your strategy to constantly improve.

Creation of Apps or Software:

Develop mobile applications or software and sell them on app stores.

Creating an application or software can be a complex process, and there are many ways to approach it. Below, I present 30 ways explained in detail for app or software creation:

Native Mobile Development: Create applications using specific languages and tools for each platform, such as Swift for iOS and Java/Kotlin for Android.

Progressive Web Apps (PWA): Develop web applications that behave like native apps on mobile devices.

Low-Code Development Tools: Use platforms that allow creating applications with less code, speeding up the development process.

No-Code Development Tools: Use platforms that allow creating applications without writing a single line of code.

Hybrid Applications: Use frameworks like Ionic or React Native to create applications that run on multiple platforms using a single codebase.

Desktop Software Development: Create applications to run on desktop computers using technologies like Java, C#, or Python.

Cloud-Based Software Development: Build cloud-hosted applications accessible from any device with an internet connection.

Open-Source Software: Contribute to or use open-source projects to develop software applications.

User Experience (UX) Focus: Emphasize usability and user interaction to create intuitive and engaging applications.

Integration of Analytics and Tracking: Implement analytics tools to gather valuable information about user behavior and improve the application.

Security and Privacy: Ensure data protection and user security through encryption techniques and good security practices.

Social Media Integration: Allow users to share content and connect through social media.

Cloud Services Integration: Utilize third-party services like cloud storage, push notifications, and authentication to enhance application functionality.

Thorough Testing: Conduct unit, integration, and acceptance testing to ensure the application functions correctly and without errors.

Software Versioning: Implement version control systems like Git to maintain a history of changes and facilitate teamwork.

Comprehensive Documentation: Create detailed technical documentation to help other developers understand and collaborate on the project.

Performance Optimization: Improve application performance by reducing loading times and optimizing resource usage.

Continuous Updates and Support: Provide regular updates to fix bugs and add new features.

Monetization: Plan a strategy to generate revenue through business models like advertising, in-app purchases, or subscriptions.

Regulatory Compliance: Ensure compliance with applicable regulations and laws, such as data protection (GDPR) or copyright.

SEO Optimization: If it's a web application, apply search engine optimization techniques to improve its visibility on the internet.

Localization and Internationalization: Adapt the application to work in different languages and regions.

Responsive User Interface: Design an interface that adapts to different screen sizes and devices.

Real-Time Applications: Use technologies like WebSockets or Firebase to create applications that update information in real-time.

Augmented Reality (AR) and Virtual Reality (VR): Incorporate AR or VR technologies to create immersive and engaging experiences.

Electronic Payment Integration: If applicable, implement secure payment systems for in-app purchases and transactions.

Gamification: Add game elements like rewards, achievements, and challenges to increase user engagement.

Virtual Assistants and AI: Integrate artificial intelligence and virtual assistants to enhance user interaction.

Continuous Maintenance and Updates: Monitor the application in production and perform updates to keep it running optimally.

Feedback and Continuous Improvement: Collect user feedback and use it to constantly improve the application.

Sale of Physical Products:

Open an online store and sell physical products through platforms like Shopify or Amazon.

Physical Store: Open a store in a busy and attractive location for the target audience. Provide a pleasant environment and personalized service.

Online Store: Create a virtual store where customers can browse and purchase your products from the comfort of their homes.

Local Fairs and Markets: Participate in local fairs and markets to exhibit and sell your products directly to customers.

Wholesale: Offer your products to other retail stores at lower prices for resale.

Consignment Sales: Place your products in stores and only pay for those that sell, reducing risks.

Event Sales: Participate in themed events such as festivals, concerts, or exhibitions to sell your products.

Catalog Sales: Create a printed or online catalog for customers to place orders.

Pop-Up Store: Open a temporary store in strategic locations to generate interest and urgency in purchase.

Sales through Social Media: Use platforms like Instagram, Facebook, or Pinterest to showcase your products and enable direct purchases.

Affiliate Program: Establish a program where individuals or influencers promote your products and earn commissions for each sale.

Phone Sales: Hire a sales team to contact potential customers and close sales over the phone.

Mail Order Sales: Send catalogs or samples to potential customers and allow them to place orders by mail.

Kiosk or Vending Machine Sales: Place your products in kiosks or vending machines in high-traffic areas.

Mobile Store: Create a store on wheels and take your products to different locations.

Event Partnership Sales: Associate your products with specific events or activities to increase their relevance.

Loyalty Program: Offer incentives to frequent customers to encourage them to keep buying your products.

Influencer Sales: Collaborate with influencers to promote your products to their audience.

Marketplace Sales: Rent a booth at local markets and sell your products directly.

Convenience Store Sales: Place your products in popular convenience stores.

Department Store Sales: Negotiate agreements to sell your products in large retail chains.

Third-Party Online Sales: Use e-commerce platforms like Amazon, eBay, or Etsy to sell your products.

Promotional Package Sales: Bundle your products with complementary items and offer attractive packages.

Subscription Sales: Create a subscription where customers receive your products periodically.

International Market Sales: Export your products to other countries and reach new markets.

Pharmacy or Drugstore Sales: If your products are related to health or personal care, place them in pharmacies.

Hotel or Resort Sales: Negotiate agreements with hotels or resorts to offer your products to their guests.

TV Program Sales: Participate in shopping TV programs to present your products to a wide audience.

Free Sample Sales: Offer free samples for customers to try your products and encourage them to make a purchase.

Networking Event Sales: Attend networking events to meet potential customers and close sales.

International Trade Fair Sales: Participate in international trade fairs to introduce your products globally.

Dropshipping:

Dropshipping is a business model in which an online retailer sells products to customers without physically holding inventory. Instead, the retailer purchases products directly from the manufacturer or wholesaler, and the latter takes care of shipping them directly to the customer. Here are 30 detailed ways to do dropshipping:

Research and choose a niche market: Identify a niche with high demand and low competition. You can use tools like Google Trends or Keyword Planner to research relevant trends and keywords.

Find reliable suppliers: Investigate and select suppliers that offer quality products, good prices, and a reliable shipping history. Sites like AliExpress, Oberlo, or SaleHoo can be useful for finding suppliers.

Create an online store: Use e-commerce platforms like Shopify, WooCommerce, or BigCommerce to set up your store. Customize the design and add attractive product descriptions.

Optimize your website for SEO: Ensure that your store performs well in search engines. Use relevant keywords in product descriptions and on your site's pages.

Add products to your store: Import products from your suppliers to your online store using dropshipping tools like Oberlo or Importify.

Set competitive prices: Determine product prices to be attractive to customers while still allowing you to make a profit.

Provide detailed product descriptions: Offer clear and detailed information about the products you're selling to help customers make informed decisions.

Incorporate attractive images: Use high-quality images to showcase products from different angles and perspectives.

Set up payment options: Enable secure and popular payment methods, such as PayPal, credit cards, and bank transfers.

Establish shipping and return policies: Define shipping policies, delivery times, and return procedures to keep customers well-informed.

Create a marketing strategy: Design a marketing plan that includes social media advertising, email marketing, and collaborations with influencers.

Use content marketing: Create relevant and valuable content on your blog to attract more potential customers and improve your website's search engine ranking.

Offer discounts and promotions: Use discounts, coupons, and promotions to increase the attractiveness of your products.

Provide excellent customer service: Respond promptly to customer inquiries and issues to build trust and loyalty.

Monitor inventory: Ensure that your suppliers always have sufficient stock to avoid shipping delays.

Track shipments: Keep customers informed about the status of their orders and provide tracking numbers so they can trace their shipments.

Offer free shipping: If possible, consider offering free shipping or reduced rates to attract more customers.

Conduct product testing: Before promoting a product on a large scale, conduct small tests to ensure the supplier meets quality and service expectations.

Monitor the competition: Study your competitors to identify opportunities and adjust your strategy accordingly.

Establish a rewards system for loyal customers: Implement a rewards program to encourage customer loyalty and repeat purchases.

Provide post-sale assistance: Offer support and assistance to customers after they make a purchase to ensure they're satisfied with their experience.

Collaborate with other businesses: Consider partnering with other online stores or influencers to jointly promote your products.

Analyze and track data: Use analytical tools to measure your store's performance and gain insights into your customers' behavior.

Offer quality guarantees: Ensure that your suppliers offer quality guarantees on their products to reassure customers.

Experiment with new products: Keep your store updated with new products and product lines to attract different customer segments.

Focus on design and user experience: Ensure that your online store is easy to navigate, and customers can quickly find the products they are looking for.

Optimize loading speed: Ensure that your store loads quickly to prevent customers from leaving due to long wait times.

Run paid advertising campaigns: Use online advertising, such as Google Ads or Facebook Ads, to drive traffic to your website.

Be transparent with shipping times: Clearly inform customers about estimated delivery times to avoid misunderstandings and disappointments.

Measure and constantly improve: Regularly analyze your results, identify areas for improvement, and adjust your strategy accordingly to grow your business.

Freelancing:

Freelancing is a way to work independently, offering your skills and services to clients without being tied to a long-term employer. Here are 30 detailed ways to do freelancing in different areas:

Content Writing: Write articles, blogs, ad copies, and other types of content for websites and companies. You can use platforms like Upwork or Fiverr to find clients.

Graphic Design: Create logos, infographics, illustrations, and other visual elements for brands and businesses. Use Adobe Illustrator or Canva for your designs.

Web Development: Design and develop websites for clients using languages like HTML, CSS, and JavaScript. You can use platforms like WordPress or Wix.

Translation: If you are fluent in two or more languages, offer translation services for documents, web pages, or advertising material.

Digital Marketing: Help businesses increase their online presence through digital marketing strategies such as SEO, social media, and advertising campaigns.

Video Editing and Animation: Create and edit promotional videos, tutorials, or animated content using tools like Adobe Premiere or After Effects.

Virtual Assistance: Perform administrative tasks, manage emails, and schedules for busy entrepreneurs and professionals.

Social Media Management: Manage and create content for companies' social media to increase their audience and engagement.

Transcription: Transcribe interviews, podcasts, or videos for those in need of written content.

Photography: Offer photography services for events, portraits, products, or landscapes.

Consulting: If you are an expert in a specific field, offer consulting and advice to businesses and individual clients.

Voiceover and Narration Services: If you have an attractive voice and narration skills, offer your services for narrating audiobooks, ads, and videos.

Programming: Work as a freelance programmer in languages like Python, Java, C++, or Ruby.

Project Management: Assist companies in planning and managing their projects to achieve their goals.

Creating Online Courses: If you have specialized knowledge, create online courses and sell them through platforms like Udemy or Teachable.

Interior Design: Provide interior design services for homes and offices.

Market Research: Conduct online research on specific topics for reports and articles.

Coaching Services: Offer coaching sessions in areas such as personal development, professional growth, or health.

Technical Support Services: Help troubleshoot technical issues and provide support to clients with computer difficulties.

Accounting Services: Provide accounting services and help businesses with their finances.

Mobile App Development: Create mobile applications for Android or iOS devices.

Scriptwriting: Write scripts for videos, short films, or even theatrical productions.

Animated Logo Creation: Create animated intros and logos for YouTube channels and companies.

Event Planning: Assist in organizing and planning events such as weddings, conferences, or parties.

SEO Services: Optimize websites to improve their ranking in search engines.

Fashion Design: Design clothing items and offer fashion and tailoring services.

Presentation Creation: Create professional presentations for companies and speakers.

Research Services: Conduct online research on specific topics for reports and articles.

Podcast Creation: Help others launch and produce their own podcasts.

Fitness Training Services: If you have fitness experience, offer online or in-person personal training services.

Selling Photographs:

If you are a photographer or have good photography skills, you can sell your images on stock image banks. Selling photographs can be a rewarding way to monetize your passion for photography. Here are 30 detailed ways to do it:

Stock Image Banks: Register on platforms like Shutterstock, Adobe Stock, or Getty Images to sell your photos to users worldwide.

Print Sales: Offer high-quality paper prints of your photographs and sell them through your own website or platforms like Etsy.

Custom Calendars: Create calendars with your most impressive images and sell them online or in local stores.

Greeting Cards: Design greeting cards with your photos and sell them online or in gift shops.

Photo Books: Create thematic photo books and sell them online or in specialized bookstores.

Exhibitions and Galleries: Participate in art exhibitions and local galleries to sell your photos to collectors and enthusiasts.

Interior Decoration Photos: Focus on capturing images suitable for decorating homes and offices.

Event Photography: Offer your services to photograph weddings, parties, and other social events.

Product Photography: Collaborate with small businesses to create appealing images of their products for use on websites and social media.

Local Landscape Photography: If you live in a scenic location, take photos of local landscapes and sell them as tourist souvenirs.

License Sales: Offer usage licenses for your images, allowing others to use them in specific projects.

Commercial Stock Photography: Focus on capturing images useful for commercial purposes, such as marketing and advertising.

Themed Stock Photography: Create thematic collections of images and sell them as special packages.

Portrait Photography: Offer portrait sessions to local clients and offer additional prints as an upsell.

Collaborations with Blogs and Websites: Reach out to bloggers and websites that need high-quality photos and offer your services.

Charity Auctions: Donate some of your best photos for charity auctions to gain visibility while supporting a cause.

Pet Photography: If you have skills in capturing adorable moments of animals, offer your services to pet owners.

Wallpaper Photo Sales: Offer your images as wallpapers for computers and mobile devices.

Architecture Photography: Collaborate with architects and real estate agents to photograph buildings and properties for commercial purposes.

Subscription Sales: Create a library of images and offer monthly or yearly subscriptions for access.

Sports Photography: Cover local sports events and sell your photos to athletes, teams, or media outlets.

Wildlife Photography: If you have access to nature and wildlife, capture unique images and sell them to nature enthusiasts.

Food Photography: Collaborate with restaurants and chefs to create appetizing images of their dishes for use on menus and social media.

Historical Archive Photo Sales: If you have access to old or historical photos, sell them to museums, educational institutions, or collectors.

Fashion Photography: Work with models and designers to create images for fashion campaigns and magazines.

Travel Photography: Document your travels and sell the images to travel magazines and websites.

Aerial Photography: If you have access to drones or aircraft, offer aerial images of urban areas or natural landscapes.

Macro Photography: Capture detailed images of small objects and sell them to designers and enthusiasts.

Wedding and Pet Portrait Photography: Combine your love for photography and animals and offer portrait sessions for pets and their owners.

Tutorial and Resource Sales: If you are a photography expert, create tutorials and sell educational resources related to photography.

Online Consulting:

Offer advice and consultancy in a specific area where you are an expert.

Online consulting has gained popularity due to its convenience and the ability to reach a broader audience in different parts of the world. Here are 30 detailed ways to do online consulting:

Individual video conferencing sessions: Offer one-on-one sessions through video conferencing platforms like Zoom, Skype, or Google Meet.

Group webinars: Organize webinars for larger groups where you can share knowledge and answer questions in real-time.

Online course creation: Design and create online courses that address specific topics and offer them to interested individuals.

Email consulting: Provide guidance through email exchanges with your clients.

Online consulting platforms: Join specialized online consulting platforms like Clarity.fm or LivePerson.

Live chat sessions: Offer real-time advice through live chat systems on your website.

Social media consulting: Utilize social media to provide tips and answer questions from your followers.

Online consulting via instant messaging: Use messaging apps like WhatsApp or Telegram to provide personalized advice.

Coaching programs: Create online coaching programs that address specific challenges and guide your clients towards their goals.

Business consulting: Offer advice to businesses in areas such as digital marketing, strategy, human resources, etc.

Health and wellness consulting: If you're an expert in health and wellness, provide personalized tips and recommendations through online platforms.

Financial advisory services: Help your clients manage their personal finances and offer investment recommendations.

Technology consulting: If you're an expert in technology, provide advice on software, hardware, or application development.

Creative consulting services: Assist clients with creative needs, such as graphic design, writing, creative marketing, etc.

Academic advising: Provide guidance to students or academics regarding their careers or research projects.

Human resources consulting: Aid individuals or companies with hiring, team management, and resolving labor conflicts.

Sales and marketing consulting: Provide strategies and tactics to improve a company's sales and marketing efforts.

Personal development consulting: Help your clients develop leadership, communication, emotional intelligence skills, etc.

Event planning advice: Offer tips and guidelines for organizing successful events.

Life and relationship consulting: Provide guidance on personal relationships and personal development.

Entrepreneurship consulting: Assist entrepreneurs in developing and launching their businesses.

Nutrition and diet consultancy: Offer personalized advice on healthy eating habits.

Social media strategy consulting: Help individuals or companies develop effective social media strategies.

Travel planning consulting: Provide personalized travel recommendations and planning.

Online learning consulting: Help businesses or individuals develop effective online courses.

Online legal advice: Provide legal advice through online platforms.

Startup human resources consulting: Assist startups in hiring and retaining talent.

Networking and cybersecurity consulting: Help individuals or companies secure their computer systems.

Gardening and landscaping consulting: Offer advice on garden design and gardening techniques.

Art and creativity consulting: Assist artists and creatives in developing their skills and finding professional opportunities.

Creating Content on YouTube:

Generate income through ads, sponsorships, and channel memberships on YouTube.

Creating content for YouTube is a versatile and exciting activity that allows you to express yourself, share your knowledge and skills, and connect with a global audience. Here are 30 detailed ways to create content on YouTube:

Tutorials: Share your expertise in a specific area and guide viewers step-by-step in performing different tasks.

Vlogs: Record your day-to-day experiences to showcase your life and personality, creating a close connection with your followers.

Product reviews: Review products relevant to your niche or industry and provide your honest opinion about them.

Interviews: Invite experts or interesting individuals to your channel and conduct in-depth interviews.

Challenges: Take on fun challenges or themed tasks and share your reactions or achievements.

Recipes and cooking: Share delicious recipes, cooking tips, and tutorials on preparing special dishes.

Travel and adventures: Document your travels and exciting activities, showcasing different places and cultures.

Tips and tricks: Offer useful tips on any topic you are knowledgeable about.

Reaction and commentary: React to viral videos or comment on popular topics, sharing your opinions and analysis.

Stories and narrations: Tell interesting or mysterious stories, whether real or fictional.

Art and crafts: Demonstrate your artistic skills and teach various crafting techniques.

Exercises and fitness: Guide your viewers through workout routines and fitness exercises.

DIY and repairs: Teach how to repair or create things on your own (Do It Yourself).

Comedy and parodies: Create humorous sketches or parodies of popular movies and TV shows.

Video games and live streams (gameplay): Play video games in real-time or share your gaming experiences.

Concerts and musical performances: Record your musical performances or share music covers and tutorials.

Curiosities and interesting facts: Present curious and unknown facts on various topics.

Style and fashion: Offer fashion tips, showcase outfits, or do shopping hauls.

Healthy lifestyle: Share tips on wellness, nutrition, and overall health.

Book discussions: Review and discuss books you've read or that are popular.

Time travel: Investigate historical events or past cultures and share your research.

Short stories: Write and narrate short stories on your channel.

Personal development: Provide advice for personal growth and skill development.

Paranormal experiences: Share stories of encounters with the paranormal or conduct investigations of haunted places.

Pop culture and fandoms: Discuss popular movies, series, comics, or books and connect with fans.

Language learning: Teach words and phrases in different languages and provide tips for learning foreign languages.

Movie and series analysis: Break down scenes, characters, and plots of movies and TV shows.

Troubleshooting and tech tutorials: Help viewers solve technical issues and offer computer tutorials.

Beauty and makeup: Share makeup tips, skincare routines, and beauty product reviews.

Movie and TV show reviews: Review movies and TV shows, offering your impressions and analysis.

Podcasting:

Create a podcast about popular topics and monetize it through advertising and sponsorships.

Define your goal: Before you start, define the purpose of your podcast. What topics do you want to cover? Who is your target audience?

Research and plan: Research other podcasts in your niche to get ideas and understand what works well. Then, plan your episodes with topics, structure, and duration.

Equipment and software: Get a good microphone, headphones, and an audio interface for optimal sound quality. Use audio editing software like Audacity or Adobe Audition to edit your episodes.

Create a script: Although some podcasts are improvised, having a script or outline will help you stay focused and ensure you cover key points.

Design a sound identity: Create distinctive intro and outro music for your podcast. You can use royalty-free music for this.

Recording the episode: Find a quiet and echo-free place to record. Avoid background noise, and ensure all participants have a good internet connection.

Audio editing: Edit the audio to remove mistakes, awkward pauses, and annoying noises. You can also add sound effects or background music.

Choose the podcast format: You can do interviews, debates, storytelling, monologues, or even mix different formats.

Branding and design: Create an attractive cover art and name that reflects the theme of your podcast.

Hosting and platform: Choose a podcast hosting service and a distribution platform like Libsyn, Podbean, or Anchor.

Upload and publish episodes: Upload your episodes to the hosting service and configure podcast information, such as description and categories.

Schedule releases: Decide how often you'll release episodes and keep a consistent schedule for your listeners.

Promote your podcast: Use social media, your website, and other platforms to promote your episodes and attract more listeners.

Build a community: Encourage interaction with your listeners through comments, emails, or social media groups.

Collaborations: Consider collaborating with other podcasters or experts in your field to expand your audience.

Feedback and analytics: Listen to listener feedback and analyze statistics to improve your podcast over time.

Adapt your focus: Be flexible and willing to adjust your podcast's focus if necessary to maintain your audience's interest.

Monetization: Explore monetization options such as advertising, sponsorships, memberships, or crowdfunding.

Co-host support: If you're more comfortable with a co-host, find someone who complements your skills and adds value to the content.

Engage the audience: Ask your listeners for their opinions or topics they'd like to hear in future episodes.

Attend podcasting events: Participate in podcasting community events to meet other creators and learn new techniques.

Adapt to different formats: Convert your episodes into other formats like transcriptions, articles, or videos to reach a broader audience.

Learn about podcast SEO: Optimize your description and titles to make your podcast more discoverable in directories and search engines.

Invite relevant guests: Invite experts or influential figures in your industry to enrich your episodes.

Mind the duration: Try to keep your episodes within an appropriate time range for your audience.

Networking: Connect with other podcasters and build relationships that may lead to future collaborations.

Evaluate and adjust your content: If certain topics or segments don't perform well, don't hesitate to change or remove them.

Thematic or special programs: Consider creating thematic or special episodes for special occasions or events.

Legality and copyright: Ensure you have the proper rights for music or any content you use in your podcast.

Have fun and be authentic: Finally, enjoy the process and show your genuine personality in each episode to connect with your audience.

Content Writing:

Writing for websites, blogs, and companies in need of content.

Pre-requisites Research: Before starting to write, research the topic at hand to ensure you have a solid understanding and informative foundation.

Define your audience: Identify your target audience and adapt your writing tone and style to meet their needs and interests.

Set a clear purpose: Define the main objective of the content. Do you want to inform, persuade, entertain, ¿or educate your readers?

Organize your content: Structure your writing into coherent paragraphs and use subtitles to facilitate reading and comprehension.

Engaging introduction: Capture the reader's attention from the beginning with an interesting introduction that presents the topic in an intriguing manner.

Content development: Expand your ideas in the body of the text, providing examples, data, statistics, or relevant case studies.

Maintain clear language: Avoid complicated jargon or unnecessary technical terms that might confuse your audience.

Use short paragraphs: Divide your ideas into short paragraphs to facilitate reading and avoid text density.

Use examples and analogies: Examples and analogies help illustrate complex concepts and make the content more accessible.

Quote reliable sources: Always back up your claims with data from trustworthy sources to gain credibility.

Apply the inverted pyramid principle: Place the most important information at the beginning and provide additional details as you progress.

Avoid redundancy: Review your writing to eliminate unnecessary repetitions and improve fluency.

Use subtitles: Subtitles help organize the content and allow readers to scan the article quickly.

Include calls to action: Incorporate calls to action to guide your readers to the next step, such as "download a resource" or "subscribe to the newsletter."

Include rhetorical questions: Rhetorical questions invite reflection and can maintain the reader's interest.

Editing and revision: Once you've finished writing, carefully review it to correct spelling, grammatical, and stylistic errors.

Use lists: Numbered or bulleted lists are effective for presenting information concisely and in an organized manner.

Stories and anecdotes: Incorporate relevant stories and anecdotes that can emotionally connect with your readers.

Offer solutions: If addressing problems, ensure to provide practical and applicable solutions.

Update your content: Whenever relevant, update your content to keep it fresh and accurate.

Use images: Use relevant images and graphics to enrich the content and make it more engaging.

Use bold and italics: Highlight important words or phrases to emphasize key concepts.

Avoid plagiarism: Never copy content from other authors. Always cite and give proper credit when necessary.

Be consistent with the tone: Maintain a coherent voice throughout the content to provide a consistent experience for the reader.

Keyword research: If writing for SEO, research relevant keywords to include them in your content.

Answer frequently asked questions: Identify the most common questions about the topic and make sure to address them in your content.

Optimize for scanning: Many readers scan content instead of reading it thoroughly. Use headings, bold text, and bullet points to facilitate this.

Add internal links: If you have related content on your website, link to it to provide more information to readers.

Be original: Offer unique perspectives and provide additional value to your readers.

Be concise: Avoid unnecessary elaboration, get to the point, and avoid irrelevant digressions.

Graphic Design:

Offering graphic design services to online clients.

Introduction to Graphic Design: Start with the basics, learn about the history and significance of graphic design in various industries.

Color Theory: Study the color wheel, harmonious combinations, and color psychology to understand how it affects emotions and perception.

Typography: Explore different typefaces, their appropriate uses, and how to choose the right typography for each project.

Composition: Learn how to organize visual elements in a balanced and appealing way to create a coherent design.

Graphic Design Software: Familiarize yourself with popular programs like Adobe Photoshop, Illustrator, and InDesign to create and edit graphics.

Logo Design: Explore logo design principles, from initial sketches to creating digital versions.

Branding: Understand how to create a cohesive and memorable brand identity through graphic design.

Flyer and Brochure Design: Learn how to create printed promotional materials with clear and appealing messages.

Business Card Design: Create professional cards that represent the essence of a company or individual.

Digital Illustration: Experiment with digital drawing and painting techniques to create original graphic art.

Packaging Design: Discover how to design packaging that stands out on shelves and communicates the essence of the product.

Social Media Design: Learn to create attractive and effective images for platforms like Facebook, Instagram, Twitter, etc.

Infographics: Design informative and visually appealing graphics to present data clearly and comprehensively.

Poster Design: Explore techniques for creating eye-catching posters with impactful messages.

Photo Retouching: Master image editing techniques to enhance photos and create stunning visual effects.

Editorial Design: Learn how to layout and design magazines, books, and catalogs professionally.

Web Design: Discover how to create attractive and functional web designs, considering user experience.

User Interface (UI) Design: Create intuitive and user-friendly graphical interfaces for applications and websites.

Graphic Animation: Experiment with animation to bring your designs to life and create interactive elements.

T-shirt Design: Create original graphics for printing on t-shirts and other garments.

Corporate Stationery Design: Create templates for letterheads, envelopes, invoices, and other corporate materials.

Icon Design: Learn to create clear and concise icons that represent concepts visually.

Mobile App Design: Adapt your design skills to create interfaces for mobile devices.

Mockup Creation: Learn how to present your designs professionally using realistic mockups.

3D Design: Explore three-dimensional graphic design to create impactful visual elements.

Book Cover Design: Create eye-catching covers that capture the attention of potential readers.

Event Design: Design graphic materials for events such as fairs, conferences, and parties.

Virtual Assistant:

Providing virtual assistance services to entrepreneurs and small businesses.

Creating a virtual assistant can involve different approaches and levels of complexity. Here's a list of 30 ways, explained in detail, to create a virtual assistant:

Basic voice assistant using Python and speech recognition libraries: Use libraries like SpeechRecognition and pyttsx3 to capture the user's voice and respond with predefined messages.

Voice assistant with smart light control: Add functionalities to control smart lights with voice commands using, for example, the RPi.GPIO library and IoT services like AWS IoT Core.

Rule-based chatbot assistant with Python: Create a simple chatbot using the ChatterBot library that responds to specific questions with predefined answers.

Chatbot assistant with deep learning: Utilize deep learning architectures like recurrent neural networks (RNN) or transformers to improve the chatbot's understanding and response capabilities.

Multilingual voice assistant: Expand the assistant's capabilities to understand and respond in multiple languages using multilingual speech recognition and synthesis models.

Voice assistant for healthcare: Design an assistant that can provide basic information about illnesses, symptoms, and first aid.

Voice assistant for smart home control: Integrate the assistant with smart devices like thermostats, security cameras, and appliances to control them through voice commands.

Voice assistant for language learning: Create an assistant that provides pronunciation examples, definitions, and exercises for learning different languages.

Chatbot assistant for technical support: Implement a chatbot that answers frequently asked questions and provides solutions for common technical issues.

Voice assistant with facial recognition: Add facial recognition capabilities using libraries like OpenCV to identify the user.

Voice assistant for movie or music recommendations: Utilize collaborative filtering algorithms to offer personalized recommendations to users based on their preferences.

Voice assistant for customer support: Create an assistant that can handle customer queries and provide appropriate responses, reducing the need for human intervention.

Chatbot assistant for education: Design a chatbot that can answer educational questions and provide additional resources.

Voice assistant for habit tracking: Create an assistant that helps users track and record their daily habits, such as exercise, diet, and sleep.

Voice assistant for meditation and well-being: Design an assistant that guides users through meditation exercises and relaxation techniques.

Chatbot assistant for psychological support: Implement a chatbot that can provide emotional support and resources for coping with stress and anxiety.

Voice assistant for flight/hotel search and booking: Integrate flight and hotel search services, allowing users to make reservations through voice commands.

Chatbot assistant for task scheduling and reminders: Create a chatbot that allows users to schedule tasks and receive reminders via text messages.

Voice assistant for expense and budget tracking: Develop an assistant that helps users keep track of their expenses and set a budget.

Voice assistant for package tracking and shipments: Integrate package tracking services, allowing users to track their shipments by simply asking.

Chatbot assistant for solving crosswords or riddles: Design a chatbot that assists users in solving crosswords and riddles by providing clues and hints.

Voice assistant for news and current events: Implement an assistant that provides updated news summaries based on the user's preferences.

Chatbot assistant for interactive machine learning: Create a chatbot that teaches the basics of machine learning and allows users to interact with trained models.

Voice assistant for cooking recipes: Design an assistant that provides recipes and guides users step-by-step during the cooking process.

Chatbot assistant for style and fashion tips: Implement a chatbot that offers fashion and style advice based on the user's preferences.

Voice assistant for physical workouts: Create an assistant that guides users through exercise routines and provides training tips.

Chatbot assistant for job search: Design a chatbot that helps users find job opportunities and provides interview tips.

Voice assistant for music learning: Implement an assistant that teaches music theory, provides practical lessons, and answers music-related questions.

Voice assistant for health and wellness tracking: Design an assistant that tracks health data, such as heart rate and sleep quality, and provides recommendations for overall well-being.

Chatbot assistant for game role-playing: Create a chatbot that allows users to engage in interactive role-playing games using text commands.

Sale of Arts and Crafts:

If you are creative, you can sell your creations on platforms like Etsy.

Own online store: Create an online store using platforms like Shopify or WooCommerce. Upload photos and detailed descriptions of your handmade products.

Online markets: Sell your crafts on sites like Etsy, ArtFire, or Handmade at Amazon, where there is an audience interested in handmade products.

Social media: Use Instagram, Facebook, and Pinterest to showcase your creations, interact with customers, and direct them to your online store.

Fairs and local markets: Reserve a booth at craft fairs or local markets to showcase and sell your products directly to the public.

Workshops and classes: Offer classes to teach your craft techniques, which can generate additional income and attract interested customers.

Selling in physical stores: Contact local stores that might be interested in selling your handmade products on consignment or wholesale.

Corporate gifts: Promote your crafts as unique and personalized gifts for companies and corporate events.

Online auctions: Participate in online auction sites like eBay, where you can sell your crafts to the highest bidder.

Craft subscription boxes: Create subscription boxes with new craft projects each month and offer them to your customers.

Collaborations with bloggers and influencers: Work with influential people to promote your products and reach a wider audience.

Wholesale: If your crafts are popular, consider selling wholesale to other stores and boutiques.

Consignment in stores: Place your products on consignment in local or relevant theme stores.

Seasonal fair sales: Participate in fairs and festivals held on special occasions, such as Christmas or Halloween.

Online second-hand sales: If you have products that don't sell well, consider selling them on online second-hand stores.

Creation of a blog or tutorial website: Generate traffic by sharing tutorials and guides on craft techniques and promote your products through the site.

Sale of patterns and prints: If you create digital patterns or designs, sell them online so others can make their own crafts.

Craft event organization: Hold workshops or events to attract people interested in learning and buying products.

Sale in local art stores: Research local art stores and galleries where you can exhibit and sell your creations.

Participation in contests and exhibitions: Enter your crafts in contests and exhibitions to increase the visibility of your work.

Create a promotional video: Make a short video showcasing your products and share it on video platforms like YouTube.

Partnerships with wedding and event companies: Offer your services to create custom crafts for weddings and other special events.

Sale in art consortia: Some communities have artist consortia or cooperatives where you can exhibit and sell your creations.

Email campaigns: Create a mailing list and send periodic newsletters with special offers and updates about your products.

Sale of craft kits: Package materials and tools needed to make a specific craft and sell them as kits.

Custom commissions: Accept client commissions to create personalized pieces according to their specifications.

Sale in international markets: Expand your reach by selling your products internationally through online stores or international markets.

Partnership with local gift shops: Place your products in local gift shops to let more people discover your creations.

Sale in natural product stores: If your crafts have an ecological or natural focus, look for stores that share this philosophy.

Affiliate programs: Create an affiliate program where others can promote your products and earn a commission on sales.

Gift cards: Offer gift cards that customers can purchase and give to others to choose their favorite products.

Online Education:

Become an online tutor or teacher and teach various subjects.

Online learning platforms: Use dedicated educational platforms such as Moodle, Canvas, Edmodo, or Google Classroom to create and manage online courses.

Real-time video conferencing: Organize virtual class sessions using tools like Zoom, Microsoft Teams, or Google Meet to interact with students live.

Recorded classes: Record your classes in video format and allow students to watch them at any time, facilitating asynchronous learning.

Discussion forums: Create forums where students can discuss topics and collaboratively solve doubts.

Webinars and virtual talks: Invite experts or conduct online presentations to enrich the course content.

Interactive multimedia content: Use images, videos, infographics, and other interactive resources to make learning more engaging.

Online assessments: Use online assessment tools like quizzes and exams to measure students' progress.

Virtual tutoring: Provide individual or small group tutoring through video conferencing to offer personalized support.

Gamification: Incorporate gaming elements such as rewards and scores to motivate students and make the learning process fun.

Virtual reality and augmented reality: Explore the use of virtual reality and augmented reality technologies to create immersive learning experiences.

Educational social networks: Create dedicated social media groups for the course to encourage collaboration and knowledge exchange among students.

Digital libraries: Facilitate access to academic resources through digital libraries and online databases.

Educational mobile apps: Develop educational apps that students can use on their mobile devices to study anywhere.

Accessible content design: Ensure that the course content is accessible to students with visual or hearing impairments.

Artificial intelligence and machine learning: Use AI to personalize the learning experience and provide content recommendations to students.

Digital portfolios: Encourage students to create digital portfolios to showcase their progress and achievements in the course.

Surveys and feedback: Gather feedback from students through online surveys to continuously improve the course.

Online collaborative projects: Foster teamwork and collaboration through projects that students work on together using online tools.

Flipped classroom: Students study the material beforehand, and during the virtual class, the focus is on discussions and addressing doubts.

Infographics and mind maps: Use online tools to create infographics and mind maps that summarize key concepts.

Educational podcasts: Create educational audio content that students can listen to while on the go or engaging in other activities.

Immersive learning experiences: Utilize virtual reality tools or virtual tours to simulate visits to specific places or real-world situations.

Massive Open Online Courses (MOOCs): Offer massive online courses to reach a broader and more diverse audience.

Progress tracking systems: Implement systems that allow students and educators to monitor their progress and performance in the course.

Online mentoring programs: Create opportunities for students to be mentors or be mentored by other professionals online.

Adaptive learning: Use platforms and tools that adapt to each student's level of knowledge and learning pace.

Integration of external resources: Link to websites, articles, and other online resources to expand the course content.

Virtual laboratories: Use simulations and virtual labs for practical experiences in scientific and technical disciplines.

Online events: Organize conferences, webinars, and virtual educational fairs to enrich the learning experience.

Online learning communities: Create online spaces where students can interact and learn from each other beyond the virtual classroom.

E-commerce for Used Products:

Sell second-hand items on specialized websites.

Choose a platform: Decide which platform you will use to create your online store. Some popular options are Shopify, WooCommerce (for WordPress), Magento, or BigCommerce.

Research the competition: Study other e-commerce stores for used products to understand how they operate and what strategies they use.

Define your niche: Focus on a specific niche of used products instead of trying to sell everything. You could specialize in used books, vintage clothing, refurbished electronics, etc.

Regulations and laws: Research the regulations and laws applicable to the sale of used products in your country or region.

Cleaning and conditioning: Ensure that the products are in good condition before putting them up for sale. Clean them and, if necessary, make minor repairs.

Quality photographs: Take clear and high-quality photos of each product to show its real condition to customers.

Detailed descriptions: Provide complete and accurate descriptions of each item, including any defects or wear.

Competitive pricing: Research the prices of similar products in the market to offer competitive and attractive prices.

Implement an efficient search system: Ensure that customers can easily search for products by category, brand, condition, etc.

Secure payment methods: Offer reliable and secure payment options, such as credit cards, PayPal, or other payment gateways.

Shipping and logistics: Establish clear shipping policies and choose logistics options that allow you to ship products quickly and safely.

Return policy: Define a fair and transparent return policy to build trust with your customers.

Feedback and reviews: Implement a review and rating system so that customers can share their experiences with other users.

Promotions and discounts: Offer promotions and discounts to attract new customers and encourage repeat purchases.

Content marketing: Create a blog or news section to share useful information about the products you sell and keep users engaged.

Social media: Use social media to promote your products and create a follower community.

Email marketing: Collect emails from customers and potential buyers to send them special offers and updates about your store.

Affiliate program: Implement an affiliate program so others can promote your products in exchange for commissions.

Collaborations and partnerships: Seek partnerships with other companies or influencers to expand your reach.

Live chat: Offer real-time assistance through live chat to resolve customer inquiries or issues.

Mobile optimization: Ensure that your website is fully functional and appealing on mobile devices.

Google Analytics: Use this tool to analyze your website's traffic and gain insights into user behavior.

Offer guarantees: If possible, provide warranties to give additional confidence to customers.

Loyalty program: Create a loyalty program that rewards frequent customers with discounts or other benefits.

Cross-selling and upselling: Suggest related or higher-value products to customers while they shop.

Sustainable packaging: Use eco-friendly packaging and promote environmentally friendly practices.

Special events and sales: Organize events or special sales to generate interest and boost sales.

Customer segmentation: Divide your customers into different groups based on their interests and behavior to personalize your offers.

Automation: Use automation tools to manage inventory, process orders, and send notifications to customers.

Exceptional customer service: Provide excellent customer service to gain the trust and loyalty of your buyers.

Forex and Cryptocurrency Trading:

Investing and trading in the foreign exchange or cryptocurrency market.

Forex:

Forex trading (foreign exchange market) is a complex activity that involves the exchange of different currencies with each other. Here are 30 detailed ways to trade in the Forex market:

Fundamental Analysis: Consists of studying the economic and political fundamentals of a country to predict the direction of its currency. Factors such as interest rates, economic growth, and government policies can influence exchange rates.

Technical Analysis: Involves studying chart patterns and historical price data to predict future movements. Technical traders use tools like moving averages, Bollinger Bands, and RSI (Relative Strength Index).

Trend Trading: Based on identifying and following uptrends or downtrends on charts. Traders attempt to enter the market when the trend is developing and exit before it reverses.

Range Trading: Focuses on trading in a sideways market, buying at support levels and selling at resistance levels.

Breakout Trading: Traders look for moments when the price breaks out of an established range, which could indicate a new trend.

Scalping: Involves making quick and frequent trades to profit from small price movements in a short period.

Hedging: Used to protect an existing position against adverse price movements by opening an opposite position in the same currency pair.

News Trading: Involves trading based on significant economic events and announcements that can affect exchange rates.

Algorithmic Trading: Relies on computer algorithms to automatically execute trades based on predefined criteria.

Social Trading: Involves automatically copying the trades of more experienced traders through social trading platforms.

Carry Trade Strategy: Traders seek to profit from interest rate differences between two currencies by holding a position for an extended period.

Correlation Strategy: Based on analyzing the relationship between currency pairs and making trading decisions based on their movements.

Seasonal Trading: Focuses on recurring historical patterns associated with certain seasons or regular economic events.

Fibonacci Trading: Uses Fibonacci retracement and extension levels to identify potential price reversal points.

MACD Divergences: Traders look for discrepancies between the MACD indicator and price to identify trend changes.

Volatility Breakout Systems: Rely on entering the market when volatility increases significantly.

Multiple Moving Averages Strategy: Uses different moving averages to identify entry or exit signals.

Trendline Trading: Focuses on drawing trendlines on charts to identify key support and resistance levels.

Candlestick Pattern Trading: Traders look for specific candlestick patterns that may indicate future price movements.

RSI Indicator Trading: Based on using the RSI indicator to identify overbought or oversold conditions in the market.

Ichimoku Indicator Trading: Uses the Ichimoku indicator to identify trends, support, and resistance levels.

Parabolic SAR Indicator Trading: Relies on the Parabolic SAR indicator to identify trend reversal points.

ADX Indicator Trading: Uses the ADX indicator to measure the strength of a trend.

Stochastic Oscillator Indicator Trading: Based on the Stochastic Oscillator indicator to identify overbought or oversold conditions.

ATR Indicator Trading: Uses the ATR indicator to measure market volatility.

Multiple Moving Averages Crossover Strategy: Uses different moving averages crossovers as entry or exit signals.

Triangle Breakout Trading: Based on triangle patterns on charts to identify breakout points.

OCO (One-Cancels-the-Other) Order Trading: Uses OCO orders to simultaneously set a profit target and a stop-loss order.

Volume Analysis Trading: Relies on volume analysis to confirm price movements.

Mean Reversion Strategy: Uses the assumption that prices tend to revert to a historical average, which can create trading opportunities.

Cryptocurrencies:

Initial Research: Investigate existing cryptocurrencies and their underlying technology (blockchain). Understanding how they work will give you a solid foundation to create your own.

Objective and Use Case: Define the purpose of your cryptocurrency and the problem it will solve. Determine its use case, whether it's for payments, utility tokens, etc.

Consensus and Algorithm: Decide on the consensus algorithm you will use to validate transactions (e.g., Proof of Work, Proof of Stake, etc.).

Technical Specifications: Define the technical specifications of your cryptocurrency, including block size, transaction speed, maximum supply, etc.

Platform Choice: Decide whether you will build your own blockchain from scratch or use an existing platform like Ethereum or Binance Smart Chain.

Programming Language: If you are developing your blockchain from scratch, choose the appropriate programming language, such as C++, Python, or Solidity.

Code Development: Begin developing the code for your cryptocurrency, making sure to follow best practices for secure development.

Security: Implement strong security measures to protect your blockchain against malicious attacks.

Genesis Block Creation: Define the genesis block of your blockchain, which will be the first block in the chain.

Network Testing: Perform thorough testing on a test network to ensure that everything works correctly.

Wallet and Explorer: Create a wallet for your cryptocurrency, both desktop and mobile versions, and a block explorer for users to track transactions.

Token Creation (if applicable): If your cryptocurrency will be token-based, define and create the tokens using a standard like ERC-20 (Ethereum).

Marketing and Community: Start building a community around your cryptocurrency and promote it to attract users and investors.

Regulations and Compliance: Ensure compliance with financial and privacy regulations that may apply to your cryptocurrency.

Launch: Officially launch your cryptocurrency, making sure all technical and security aspects are in place.

Exchanges Listing: Negotiate with exchanges to have your cryptocurrency listed on their trading platform.

Mining or Validation: If you use Proof of Work, allow miners to join the network and earn rewards for validating transactions.

Nodes and Decentralization: Encourage the creation of nodes to increase decentralization and security of your network.

Updates and Improvements: Establish a plan for future updates and improvements based on community feedback.

Technical Support: Provide technical support to users and miners to resolve issues and enhance the overall experience.

Rewards Program: Consider implementing rewards programs to incentivize the use and adoption of your cryptocurrency.

Smart Contracts (if applicable): If using a platform like Ethereum, consider developing smart contracts for specific use cases.

Security Audit: Conduct a security audit to ensure your cryptocurrency is protected against vulnerabilities.

Developer Adoption: Attract developers to create applications and services on your blockchain.

Governance: Define a governance model that allows the community to vote and make decisions about the future of the cryptocurrency.

Partnerships and Alliances: Seek opportunities to establish partnerships with other companies or projects that can drive adoption of your cryptocurrency.

Education and Documentation: Provide detailed documentation and educational materials to help users and developers understand how your cryptocurrency works.

Scalability: Plan and address scalability issues as the network and user base grow.

Feedback and Continuous Improvement: Listen to community feedback and make continuous improvements to maintain the relevance of your cryptocurrency.

Ongoing Legal Compliance: Ensure ongoing compliance with financial regulations as they evolve.

Influencer:

Building an audience on social media and working with brands to promote their products or services.

Find Your Passion: Identify a topic or niche that you are passionate about and have knowledge or experience to share.

Define Your Audience: Determine who you want to target as an influencer. Knowing your audience will help you create relevant and engaging content.

Choose Your Platforms: Research and select the most suitable social media platforms for your niche, such as Instagram, YouTube, TikTok, Twitter, or LinkedIn.

Create a Content Calendar: Plan your posts in advance to maintain a consistent and coherent presence on social media.

Develop Your Style: Find your unique voice and style to differentiate yourself from other influencers in your niche.

Content Quality: Prioritize quality over quantity. Create engaging, well-produced, and valuable content for your audience.

Interact with Your Audience: Respond to comments and messages from your followers. Interaction is key to building a loyal community.

Collaborate with Other Influencers: Collaborate with other influencers in your niche to increase your visibility and reach new audiences.

Use Hashtags Strategically: Research relevant hashtags in your niche and use them in your posts to expand your reach.

Apply SEO in Your Posts: Optimize your titles and descriptions with relevant keywords to improve your visibility in platform internal searches.

Brand Consistency: Maintain a consistent visual appearance across all your platforms, from your profile picture to the colors and filters you use.

Participate in Events and Conferences: Attend events related to your niche to meet other industry professionals and expand your network.

Offer Exclusive Content: Provide exclusive content or previews to your followers to encourage their loyalty.

Organize Giveaways and Contests: Host giveaways and contests to incentivize your followers to participate and share your content.

Analyze Your Metrics: Use platform analytics tools to understand which content performs best and adjust your strategy accordingly.

Be Authentic: Show your personality and authenticity in your posts. Authenticity connects with the audience.

Explore New Trends: Stay up-to-date with the latest trends in your niche and use them to keep your content fresh and relevant.

Create Videos and Live Streams: Videos are a powerful way to connect with your audience. Conduct live streams to interact in real-time.

Use Instagram and Facebook Stories: Stories are ideal for showing behind-the-scenes moments and creating a sense of closeness with your audience.

Collaborate with Brands and Companies: Once you have established an audience, you can collaborate with brands to promote products or services.

Share Testimonials and Reviews: Include testimonials and reviews of products you genuinely like and find useful for your audience.

Offer Tips and Tutorials: Share your knowledge through tips and tutorials that help your audience solve problems or learn something new.

Engage in Debates and Conversations: Comment on posts by other influencers and participate in debates to increase your visibility.

Use Storytelling: Share personal stories or narratives that can excite or inspire your audience.

Be Consistent and Patient: Building an audience takes time, so be patient and consistently work on your content.

Monetize Your Content: Explore options to make money with your content, such as affiliate programs, advertising, or creating digital products.

Evaluate Your Competitors: Observe other influencers in your niche and analyze which strategies work for them.

Participate in Online Communities: Join groups or forums related to your niche to interact with more people interested in your topics.

Maintain Ethics and Transparency: Be honest with your audience about any collaborations or product promotions you do.

Never Stop Learning: The digital world is constantly changing, so stay updated with new trends and tools to improve as an influencer.

Also by Arthur Anderson

Las Mejores 20 Ideas para Ganar Dinero en Internet
Travesía Cósmica: Explorando los Límites del Universo"
El Misterio de El Risco Tenebroso: Secretos, Sacrificio y Redención
"The Mystery of the Dark Cliff: Secrets, Sacrifice, and Redemption"
Cosmic Journey: Exploring the Boundaries of the Universe
Las Mejores Ideas de Inversión con Poco Dinero y Buen Resultado
The Best 20 Ideas for Making Money Online
The Best Low-Capital Investment Ideas with Good Results
Henrik and the Ghost Island: The Legend of Zimbha Nau
Treasures and Betrayals: In Search of the Isle of Death
Henrik y la Isla Fantasma: La Leyenda de Zimbha Nau
Los Espíritus de Versaviz: Secretos de una Casa Antigua
Tesoros y Traiciones: En Busca de la Isla de la Muerte
The Spirits of Versaviz: Secrets of an Ancient House